*With the Help of Love,
I Can Do Anything*

With the Help of Love, I Can Do Anything

Angelo K. Menefee

VANTAGE PRESS
New York

Illustrated by John Cannizo

FIRST EDITION

All rights reserved, including the right of
reproduction in whole or in part in any form.

Copyright © 1996 by Angelo Menefee

Published by Vantage Press, Inc.
516 West 34th Street, New York, New York 10001

Manufactured in the United States of America
ISBN: 0-533-11694-5

0 9 8 7 6 5 4 3 2 1

In loving memory of the late Lawrence D. Menefee and Viola Menefee (my parents), who showed me that, with the help of love, I can do anything.

With the Help of Love, I Can Do Anything

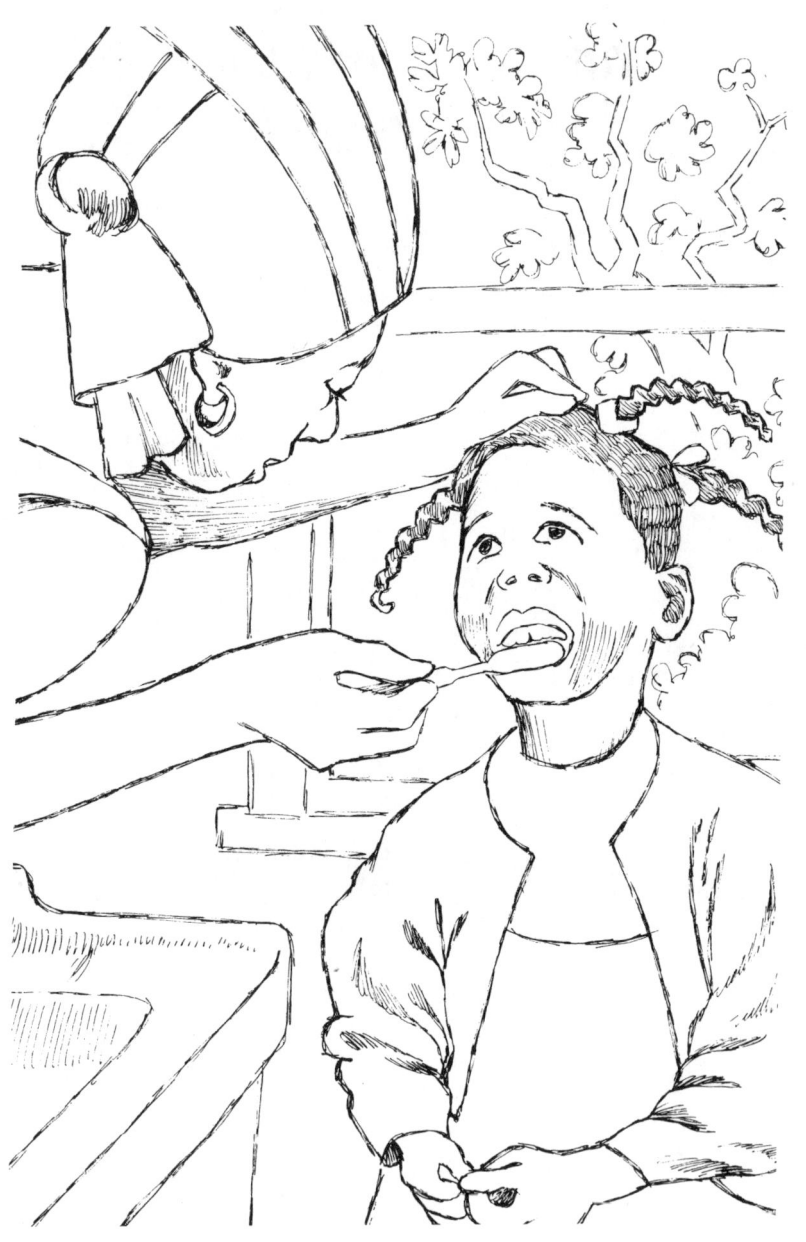

"Hello, I'm Karen. With Mommy's help, I know how to brush my teeth up and down while looking in the mirror. See?"

"Hello, I'm Debbie. With Daddy's help I learned how to wash my face, ears, arms, and legs. When I am done, he holds his arms out and he says, 'My big girl!' "

"Hello, I'm Brian. With Mommy's help, I learned how to put my shirt and pants on the right way. First, I look at the tag that goes in the back."

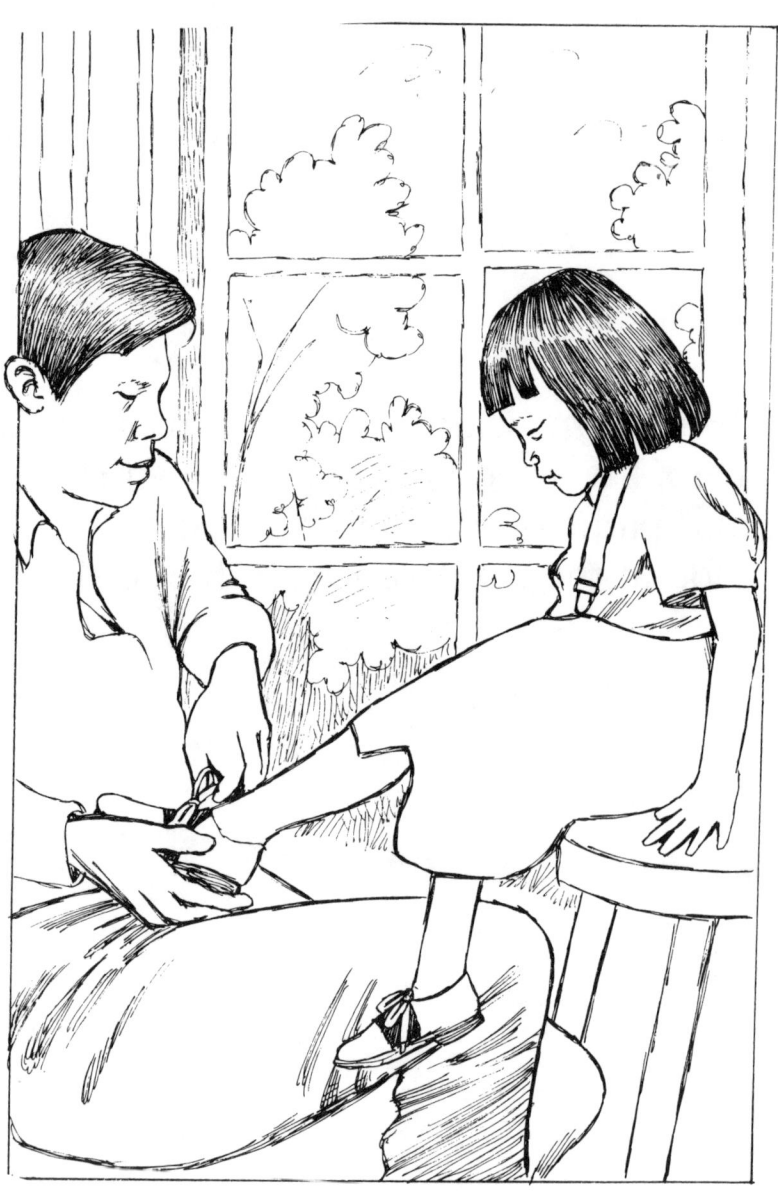

"Hello, I'm Brian. With Mommy's help, I learned how to put my shirt and pants on the right way. First, I look at the tag that goes in the back."

"Hello, my name is Kim. With the help of Daddy, I learned how to put my shoes on the right feet. Of course, I put them side by side first!"

"Hi! I am Jenny. And now I am ready to eat breakfast. Daddy and Mommy helped me learn how to say grace at the table."

"Hi, my name is Sikia. I am ready to go to school. My mother walks me and shows me how to cross the street. She points to the light. Green means GO, red means STOP, and yellow means WAIT!"

"Hello, my name is Roger. My mommy and daddy told me to raise my hand in school when I have something to say and to obey the teacher."

"Hi, my name is Mary. Mommy and Daddy told me to wait at the gate when school is over until Daddy picks me up, and not to talk to strangers. We have a password."

"Hello, my name is Billy. When I get home, I can't wait to do my homework, with Daddy's help, at the table while Mommy is cooking dinner."

"Hi! My name is Kaitlyn. After homework and dinner, my mom and dad let me look at TV until I fall asleep with my cat, Fluffy."

"Hi! I'm Bobby. My mommy and daddy help me put on my night clothes. Mom and Dad taught me how to say my prayers beside the bed."

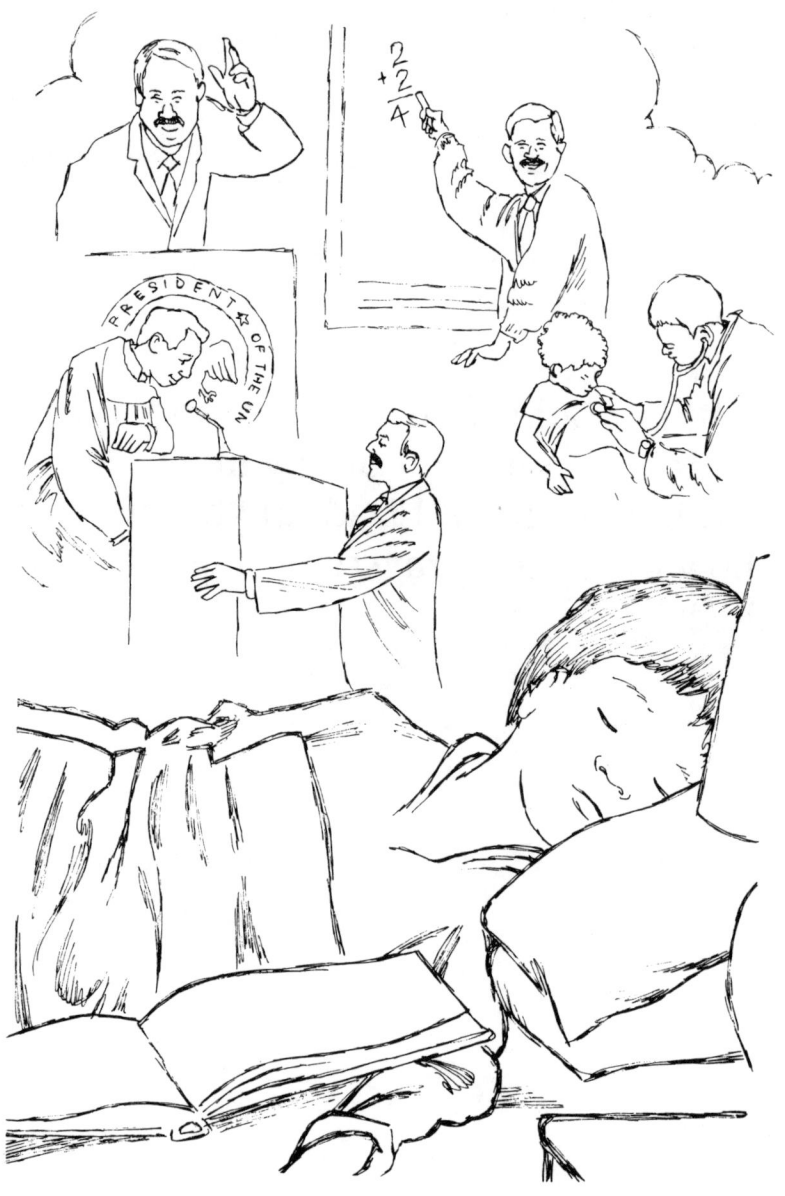

"Hello, I'm Raymond. Once in bed, I dream of all the things I did today and all that I can become. With the help of LOVE, I can do anything and become anybody like a lawyer, president, a judge, a teacher, or even maybe a surgeon!"